Handbook for North Carolina Mayors and Council Members

David M. Lawrence

UNC
SCHOOL OF
GOVERNMENT

The School of Government at the University of North Carolina at Chapel Hill works to improve the lives of North Carolinians by engaging in practical scholarship that helps public officials and citizens understand and improve state and local government. Established in 1931 as the Institute of Government, the School provides educational, advisory, and research services for state and local governments. The School of Government is also home to a nationally ranked graduate program in public administration and specialized centers focused on information technology and environmental finance.

As the largest university-based local government training, advisory, and research organization in the United States, the School of Government offers up to 200 courses, webinars, and specialized conferences for more than 12,000 public officials each year. In addition, faculty members annually publish approximately 50 books, manuals, reports, articles, bulletins, and other print and online content related to state and local government. Each day that the General Assembly is in session, the School produces the *Daily Bulletin Online*, which reports on the day's activities for members of the legislature and others who need to follow the course of legislation.

The Master of Public Administration Program is offered in two formats. The full-time, two-year residential program serves up to 60 students annually. In 2013 the School launched MPA@UNC, an online format designed for working professionals and others seeking flexibility while advancing their careers in public service. The School's MPA program consistently ranks among the best public administration graduate programs in the country, particularly in city management. With courses ranging from public policy analysis to ethics and management, the program educates leaders for local, state, and federal governments and nonprofit organizations.

Operating support for the School of Government's programs and activities comes from many sources, including state appropriations, local government membership dues, private contributions, publication sales, course fees, and service contracts. Visit www.sog.unc.edu or call 919.966.5381 for more information on the School's courses, publications, programs, and services.

Michael R. Smith, Dean
Thomas H. Thornburg, Senior Associate Dean
Frayda S. Bluestein, Associate Dean for Faculty Development
L. Ellen Bradley, Associate Dean for Programs and Marketing
Todd A. Nicolet, Associate Dean for Operations
Ann Cary Simpson, Associate Dean for Development
Bradley G. Volk, Associate Dean for Administration

FACULTY

Whitney Afonso	Richard D. Ducker	Christopher B.	Jessica Smith
Trey Allen	Joseph S. Ferrell	McLaughlin	Meredith Smith
Gregory S. Allison	Alyson A. Grine	Kara A. Millonzi	Carl W. Stenberg III
David N. Ammons	Norma Houston	Jill D. Moore	John B. Stephens
Ann M. Anderson	Cheryl Daniels Howell	Jonathan Q. Morgan	Charles Szypszak
A. Fleming Bell, II	Jeffrey A. Hughes	Ricardo S. Morse	Shannon H. Tufts
Maureen Berner	Willow S. Jacobson	C. Tyler Mulligan	Vaughn Mamlin Upshaw
Mark F. Botts	Robert P. Joyce	Kimberly L. Nelson	Aimee N. Wall
Michael Crowell	Kenneth L. Joyner	David W. Owens	Jeffrey B. Welty
Sara DePasquale	Diane M. Juffras	LaToya B. Powell	Richard B. Whisnant
Leisha DeHart-Davis	Dona G. Lewandowski	William C. Rivenbark	
Shea Riggsbee Denning	Adam Lovelady	Dale J. Roenigk	
James C. Drennan	James M. Markham	John Rubin	

© 2013
School of Government
The University of North Carolina at Chapel Hill

Printed in the United States of America

19 18 17 16 15   3 4 5 6 7

ISBN 978-1-56011-738-4

♾ This publication is printed on permanent, acid-free paper in compliance with the North Carolina General Statutes.

 Printed on recycled paper

About the Series

Local Government Board Builders offers local elected leaders practical advice on how to effectively lead and govern. Each of the booklets in this series provides a topic overview, and many offer specific tips on effective practice, worksheets, and reflection questions, to help local elected leaders improve their work. The series focuses on common activities for local governing boards, such as selecting and appointing committees and advisory boards, planning for the future, making better decisions, improving board accountability, and effectively engaging stakeholders in public decisions.

Vaughn Mamlin Upshaw, lecturer in public administration and government at the UNC School of Government, is the series editor.

Other Books in the Series

Leading Your Governing Board: A Guide for Mayors and County Board Chairs, Vaughn Mamlin Upshaw, 2009

A Model Code of Ethics for North Carolina Local Elected Officials, A. Fleming Bell, II, 2010

Creating and Maintaining Effective Local Government Citizen Advisory Committees, Vaughn Mamlin Upshaw, 2010

Working with Nonprofit Organizations, Margaret Henderson, Lydian Altman, Suzanne Julian, Gordon P. Whitaker, and Eileen R. Youens, 2010

Public Outreach and Participation, John B. Stephens, Ricardo S. Morse, and Kelley T. O'Brien, 2011

Local Government Revenue Sources in North Carolina, Kara A. Millonzi, 2011

Getting the Right Fit: The Governing Board's Role in Hiring a Manager, Vaughn Mamlin Upshaw, John A. Rible IV, and Carl W. Stenberg, 2011

The Property Tax in North Carolina, Christopher B. McLaughlin, 2012

Local Government Budgeting: A Guide for North Carolina Elected Officials, Julie M. Brenman, with Gregory S. Allison, 2013

Suggested Rules of Procedure for the Board of County Commissioners, Joseph S. Ferrell, Third Edition, 2002

Suggested Rules of Procedure for Small Local Government Boards, A. Fleming Bell, II, Second Edition, 1998

Suggested Rules of Procedure for a City Council, A. Fleming Bell, II, Third Edition, 2000

Contents

Preface

This handbook is intended for elected officials in North Carolina cities and towns, and for persons interested in or seeking election to municipal office. It may also be helpful to citizens interested in a short introduction to North Carolina cities.

The first part of the handbook explores the nature of cities and towns in North Carolina, including how they come into existence, how they are run, what they may and must do, and how they are financed. The second part focuses on the work of the mayor and council, covering organization of the council, council meetings and action, and potential liabilities of a mayor or council member.

The handbook is introductory in nature and, as a result, treats its subjects without a great amount of detail. For readers interested in further information, a list of more detailed School of Government publications is set out in Appendix 2.

David M. Lawrence
William Rand Kenan, Jr., Professor of Public Law
 and Government, Emeritus
Chapel Hill
September 2013

PART 1
The Nature, Structure, and Functions of City Government

1 The Nature of the City

The word "city" describes at least two entities: one physical or geographical, the other legal. The physical city is a place, an urban community, whose boundaries—constantly changing—are defined by patterns of land use, of commuting, of economic dependence. The legal city is a governmental entity whose boundaries are defined by law. Although these two sorts of cities overlap, they are almost never identical. In some cases, more frequently in small communities, the physical city exists alone. More often, the physical city outgrows its legal counterpart, and sometimes several legal cities share governmental responsibility in a single urban community. This handbook's concern is the legal city.

Its Corporate Form

In law, a city is a "municipal corporation." A corporation is, under the law, a "person" (an artificial one, to be sure), an entity separate from its owners. In this respect a municipal corporation is no different from a business corporation, and the benefits that cause businesses to organize into corporations motivate city governments to do so as well. Among these benefits are, first, the fact that a corporation continues in existence without regard to changes in its ownership. Owners may die or leave the corporation and new owners may join, but the corporation's existence continues unaffected. This attribute facilitates long-term projects and commitments by the enterprise, whether it is a manufacturing company or a city. Second, the corporate form permits a limited commitment of assets by the owners; the corporation must meet its obligations from its own resources, not those of its owners. The owners' liability is limited—to the amount of their investment in business corporations, by tax rate limits in municipal corporations. Third, the corporate form facilitates the delegation of management responsibility from the corporation's owners to its board of directors or governing board and administration.

Most business corporations are organized for economic purposes with the intention of returning a profit to their owners—their shareholders. Municipal corporations, on the other hand, are part of the governmental structure of the state, organized to provide public services and regulate activities in a specific community. Perhaps the most notable difference between municipal corporations and business corporations lies in the involuntary character of "ownership" of the former. A person becomes an owner—a stockholder—of a business corporation by the voluntary act of purchasing that corporation's stock. But a person joins a municipal corporation involuntarily. This corporation's owners include everyone who lives within its borders, and the only way one can escape ownership is to move away.

Creation, Abolition, Growth

Incorporation

In North Carolina, a city may be established—that is, incorporated—only by act of the General Assembly.[1] The decision to incorporate a community is essentially a political one; the General Assembly is not bound by any standards of population density, development, or tax base. It may incorporate an area with only a few residents or with a largely rural character; it may even incorporate an area in anticipation of development, before any sort of town actually exists. When the General Assembly incorporates an area, it may do so immediately or it may first require the approval of the area's residents. The decision whether to require voter approval rests exclusively with the General Assembly; local voters have no inherent constitutional right to approve such an incorporation.

In North Carolina, a city may be established—that is, incorporated—only by act of the General Assembly.

The General Assembly typically incorporates a few cities each legislative session, either directly or subject to a referendum. At the beginning of 2013, there were 553 active incorporated cities and towns in North Carolina.

Abolition

Small towns are sometimes the reflection of ruined hopes. Most frequently, the principal local industry has closed down and moved away, and many of the residents soon follow. Often the town's leaders are among those who leave, and the town government simply withers away. An election date comes and goes, and no one files for the town board; the

---

1. During two periods during the twentieth century, a handful of North Carolina cities were incorporated by action of the Municipal Board of Control, a state administrative agency. That board no longer exists.

incumbents continue to meet for a time, and then they stop. The legal town becomes inactive, and then it dies. The law, however, usually lags behind fact, as evidenced by the lack of an organized method in law for abolishing town governments that have ceased to exist in fact. Abolition can be effected only by the General Assembly, and it acts only on request. A 1971 act repealed the charters of ninety-five inactive towns, but another sixty or so still exist—ghosts of old dreams.

Annexation

Urban communities grow, perhaps more often than they decline, and the legal city usually is interested in expanding its boundaries to keep pace with that growth. For half a century, North Carolina law facilitated the growth of city boundaries through an annexation procedure that left decision making in the hands of the city council and not the residents or property owners of the area being annexed. State law changed, however, in 2011, and annexation is currently much more difficult. As a practical matter, two methods of annexation are now available to North Carolina cities. First, a city may annex territory—whether adjacent to or up to three miles from the existing city limits—if petitioned to do so by all the real property owners in the area. Second, the General Assembly may always expand—or contract—the boundaries of a city.

City, Town, Village

Thus far, this handbook has used the term "city" to refer to incorporated municipal governments in North Carolina. That is the term used to refer to those governments by the principal statewide law affecting municipal government. A majority of these governments, however, are officially "towns," and a very few are "villages." The terms used are interchangeable in North Carolina, with no effect on the powers held by a particular city, town, or village. While the size of a place commonly determines whether it is a city, town, or village, there are no established rules of terminology in North Carolina; rather, local preference prevails. The Town of Cary, for example, has more than 135,000 residents, while the City of Saluda has around 700. Therefore, purely for the sake of convenience, this handbook will continue to refer to *cities*, with the understanding that towns and villages are also included.

2 Cities in the Intergovernmental Context

Cities in North Carolina share governmental responsibilities with the federal, state, and county governments and with a variety of special-purpose local governments. It is rare for any function to entirely be the responsibility of any one of these levels or types of governments. Rather, the pattern is one of shared responsibilities—for policy making, for operations, for financing. Take streets and highways as an example. Construction and maintenance is, in North Carolina, the operational responsibility of the state and the cities. These two levels of government also share the financing of this function, but so do the federal government and, to a very small extent, county government. Similar descriptions could be given for most other functions of city government; the details would differ, but the pattern of shared responsibility would remain.

Cities, then, do not exist in isolation from other forms of government. Rather, they are part of a complicated mosaic of responsibility. Determining the cities' place in this mosaic is largely the work of the General Assembly.

Cities and the General Assembly

In the partnership between state and local government in North Carolina, it is the state, more particularly the General Assembly, that is the senior partner. Cities—and other local governments—owe their very existence to the General Assembly, and the General Assembly can pretty much abolish cities at will, change their borders, modify their structures, or grant or take away their powers. In this state there is no "inherent right" of local self-government, nor is there in North Carolina the sort of "home rule" that permits cities in other states to write their own charters. Much of state government, like cities, is beholden to the General Assembly, which has broad powers to create, merge, restructure, and abolish state agencies as well as local ones. The basic framework of government in North Carolina, then—what is done by government, who does it, how it is financed—is established by General Assembly action.

Because cities gain their authority to act—to provide services, to regulate activities, to raise revenues—from the General Assembly, a city that wants to begin a new activity must be able to point to legislative authorization to do so. It is not enough (as it is with private corporations) to say that there is no prohibition on what the city wants to do; instead, the law must permit, expressly or by implication, the city to act.

The General Assembly authorizes cities to act through two general types of legislation: general laws and local acts. A general law is one that applies statewide to all cities or to all cities in a particular class, such as all cities with populations of 5,000 or more. (This latter sort of general law—the "classified" general law—is not widely used in North Carolina.) Most of the basic general laws that govern cities (see Appendix 1) were either first written or extensively revised in the latter part of the twentieth century, and they provide sufficient authority for most cities to do most of the things they might wish to.

When a city is interested in doing something new or in undertaking a familiar task in a way not permitted by general law, it may seek a local act authorizing the new power or procedure. A local act is an act of the General Assembly that applies to one specific city or county or occasionally to a few cities or counties. Under the General Assembly's courtesy system, if the delegation that represents the city or county involved supports the local bill, the rest of the legislature normally defers to the delegation's wishes and passes it. As a result, local acts are easier to enact than are general laws, and they sometimes serve the important function of permitting local experimentation on a program that could not be enacted statewide. For example, in 1967 Raleigh received authorization by local act to annex areas that were not adjacent to the city limits. Other cities received similar authority in 1969 and 1971, and in 1973 an act was passed to permit such annexations statewide.

Cities and Counties

At one time, cities and counties—the two principal types of local government in North Carolina—were viewed as being rather different creatures. Counties were understood to be subdivisions of state government, created to help administer state functions and programs. Thus county officials provided courts, registered deeds, cared for the poor, and even (in the nineteenth and early twentieth centuries) collected the state's taxes. Cities, on the other hand, were understood to be local government units in the fullest sense. They were established, usually at the behest of their residents, to provide those local services that an urbanized community needs: police and fire protection, water and sewer services, streets, and so on. From the 1930s on, counties were responsible for education, welfare, and health—"people" services needed by all North Carolina citizens regardless of where they lived. (Counties shared their responsibilities with the state and federal governments, which in fact provided most of the money for these services.) Cities, under this system, were chiefly responsible for "property" services—public safety, utilities, sanitation—needed primarily by people living in built-up communities.

In recent years, however, this traditional picture has changed. Subdivisions have been developed far from any city. When the residents of these new homes have needed urban services, they have had only their counties to turn to. Thus county governments have begun providing services once thought to be city responsibilities: fire protection, water and sewer services, recreation. In addition, the notion of what governmental services are needed by all the state's residents has broadened, and so some formerly city functions—hospitals, libraries, solid-waste disposal—have become largely the responsibility of counties. Counties have therefore retained their historical role as state subdivisions but have also become local governments in the same sense that cities are. We have reached the point where counties and cities are far more alike than not, with parallel authority to perform most of the functions of local government.

3 How a City Is Governed

The Governing Board

A city's governing board—variously called the council, the board of commissioners, or the board of aldermen—holds ultimate authority to act for the city. It decides what services the city provides and at what level. It establishes the city's fiscal policy through adopting the annual budget ordinance, and it levies the city's taxes. It adopts the city's ordinances. In addition to these sorts of broad policy-making responsibilities, a city's governing board typically decides numerous separate administrative matters. Thus it may authorize the city to enter into a contract or buy or sell a parcel of property, award the successful bid on a purchase or construction project, or accept the dedication of a street.

When it does all of these things and many others, the council must act as a collective body. Just as the city itself has a legal existence separate from its residents, so, too, is a city council a body separate from its individual members. The council members can act as a city council only when properly convened as a governing board in a legal meeting. An individual member of the council may not act on its behalf—at least not without specific authorization from the council itself. And a majority (or even the entire membership) of the council may act in the council's name only at a council meeting called and held pursuant to law. Thus it is essential that a council and its advisors know the proper way to call and hold a meeting and to take action.

The structure of each city's governing board is normally set out in the city's charter, a local act of the General Assembly that serves as a sort of "constitution" for the city. In most cases, that structure is established by legislative act (although the legislation usually follows the wishes of the city's leaders and residents), but it can also be established by act of the governing board itself or by the city's voters.

While no typical city governing board structure exists in North Carolina, these structures do fall within a relatively narrow range. Boards vary in size from two members to eleven, with the overwhelming majority having between four and six members. Terms are for either two years or four, and four-year terms are usually staggered so that about half the board is elected every two years. Most board members are elected from the city at large;

fewer than 15 percent of cities use some sort of district or ward system. Finally, almost all cities elect board members in nonpartisan elections; at the beginning of 2013, only seven cities out of a total of 553 used partisan elections. Table 3.1 contains summary figures on the structure of governing boards in North Carolina cities as of the beginning of 2013.[1]

The Mayor

North Carolina's mayors enjoy very few formal powers. With but few exceptions, these powers consist of presiding at governing board meetings, voting to break ties at those meetings (and at no other time), and signing documents on behalf of the city. The *strong mayor system* found in many of the nation's larger cities, under which the mayor is charged with actually running city government, is simply not found in this state. Despite having so few formal powers, however, many North Carolina mayors do exercise great influence in the operation of their cities. The office of mayor is viewed, by both the electorate and those who serve in city office, as the chief political office in city government, and by the force of that perception and of personality, many mayors effectively lead their governing boards. Moreover, in small towns without a manager (the role of the manager is discussed in more detail below), the mayor often serves as de facto chief administrator, simply because he or she is willing to work long hours in the town hall.

The Administration

North Carolina is a stronghold of the *council-manager form* of city government, under which the governing board appoints the city manager (and two or three other employees) and charges him or her with appointing all other employees and operating the city under the board's general supervision. The system is intended to provide professional management of the city, at the same time insulating most city employees from direct political control by the governing board. All but 10 of the 132 North Carolina cities with 5,000 or more residents operate under the council-manager plan, and just over one-half of the 200-odd cities with populations between 1,000 and 5,000 employ a manager.

A professional manager is too expensive for smaller towns, however, and so a majority of the state's municipalities operate under the *mayor-council plan*, under which all department

---

1. These figures are drawn from the School of Government webpage, "Forms of North Carolina City Government." A searchable database setting out each North Carolina city, town, or village's current form of government can be accessed at www.iog.unc.edu/pubs/FOG/index.php .

Table 3.1. North Carolina Governing Board Structures (Total Number of Cities as of January 2013 = 553)

CHARACTERISTIC	NUMBER OF CITIES
Size of Governing Board:	
11 members	1
9 members	1
8 members	11
7 members	17
6 members	59
5 members	316
4 members	111
3 members	36
2 members	1
Term of Office of Governing Board Members:	
2-Year Terms	164
4-Year Terms, Non-Staggered	35
4-Year Terms, Staggered	345
Combination 2- & 4-Year Terms	9
Mode of Election of Governing Board:	
Elected At Large	477
Elected At Large, with District Residence Requirement	23
Combination of At-Large & Election with District Residence Requirement	10
Election by and from Election Districts	17
Combination of At-Large & District Members	26
Type of Election:	
Nonpartisan	446
Partisan	7

heads report directly to the governing board. Some mayor-council towns employ a town administrator, to whom the board delegates personnel decisions. With other small towns, actual government practices frequently take forms unmentioned in the statutes. It was noted above that the mayor of such a town often acts, in fact, as its chief administrator. In addition to or sometimes instead of such an arrangement, governing board members sometimes each assume supervisory responsibility for a department of the town government, acting almost as an elected department head. Occasionally, small towns even turn to informal decision making by town meetings, with the board carrying out the wishes of the townspeople as reflected at a given meeting.

At-a-Glance: North Carolina City Functions (Excluding Budget Ordinance Adoption)

Function	Services Provided/Funding
Public Safety	• **Police Services** 　◦ Enforces state criminal law, local ordinances 　◦ Financed by local taxes, other general revenues • **Fire Protection** 　◦ Suppresses, prevents fires 　◦ Financed by local taxes, other general revenues • **Emergency Medical Services** 　◦ Provides emergency medical services at local level
Streets and Sidewalks	• **Constructs, maintains roads within city boundaries*** • **Financed from several sources, including Powell Bill funds, local taxes, other general revenues, special assessments**
Public Enterprises	• **Public Utility Services** 　◦ Water and sewerage 　◦ Electricity and gas 　◦ Solid-waste collection and disposal 　◦ Parking 　◦ Public transportation 　◦ Cemeteries 　◦ Auditoriums, coliseums, convention centers • **Often operated/provided by private entities** • **Normally financed by user charges**
Leisure/Cultural Activities	• **Parks and Recreation** 　◦ Owns/operates parks, playgrounds, programs, athletic leagues 　◦ Planning, operation often undertaken by governing board–appointed citizen commissions/boards 　◦ Financed by taxes, other general revenues
Housing and Development	• **Housing and Community Development** 　◦ Eliminates blight, provides affordable housing 　◦ Partially managed by housing authorities • **Economic Development** 　◦ Recruits new business, revitalizes downtown areas, offers worker training programs
Development Regulation	• **Land Use Regulation** 　◦ Plans, regulates how land will be used, developed, via basic comprehensive plan • **Historic Preservation and Aesthetics** 　◦ Funds local preservation groups, designates historic districts, structures
Administration	• **Central Management**　　• **Revenue Collection** • **Financial Management**　• **Human Resources** • **Purchasing**

* Indicates a duty shared with the State

4 The Functions of City Government

Once incorporated, a North Carolina city need not do much of anything. The only function that North Carolina law requires a city to perform is enforcement of the State building code, but most smaller cities and towns meet this requirement by contracting enforcement duties out to their respective counties. In addition, cities incorporated after specific dates lose their eligibility for certain state-shared revenues if they do not provide a small package of services, but if a city is willing to forfeit those revenues, there is no other legal requirement for providing services. Nevertheless, almost all cities do in fact engage in a basic set of functions: police and fire protection, street maintenance, community water and sometimes sewerage systems, and land use regulation. The larger the city, the more activities it tends to engage in. Thus a city enjoys great flexibility in deciding the functions it will undertake, the extent of and manner by which it will offer these services, and how it will finance them. This chapter briefly reviews the various activities in which the general law permits cities to participate.

Public Safety
Police Services

Almost all cities provide police services to their residents, although departments range in size from several hundred officers in the largest cities to the small town's single officer. Except in those smaller towns that provide police services by contract with the sheriff, county sheriffs' departments generally do not patrol within cities.

City police officers in North Carolina enforce both the state's criminal law and locally adopted ordinances, and their jurisdiction includes not only the city itself but also all areas within one mile of the city and all city-owned property wherever located. The state, seeking to ensure a high-quality corps of law enforcement personnel, requires that all law enforcement officers in North Carolina meet state-established training standards. Police services are normally financed with local taxes and other general revenues.

Fire Protection

As with police services, organized fire protection is available in almost all North Carolina cities. The organizational form ranges from the full-time paid departments of the larger cities to the volunteer companies—often receiving some public financial support—that protect the smaller towns. As an intermediate method, many cities supplement volunteer companies with one or more paid firefighters. The state's primary role in fire protection is to operate, through the Department of Insurance, the system that rates fire departments for insurance purposes. Cities normally finance fire protection with local taxes and other general revenues.

Fire departments exist primarily to suppress fires, but fire protection also includes preventing fires. State law directs all cities to designate their principal business districts as "primary fire limits," within which frame or wooden structures are severely restricted. Should a city not do so, the State Insurance Commissioner may act in the city's stead. In addition, the State building code includes a fire prevention code, and, as noted earlier, cities are required to assure enforcement of the building code within their respective areas.

Emergency Medical Services

Although counties have primary responsibility at the local level for emergency medical services (EMS), some cities operate EMS agencies or contribute to the support of private agencies that provide services within the area of the city.

Emergency Management Services

Although North Carolina cities may support emergency management agencies, the state's emergency management statutes give to counties primary local responsibility for this activity, and many cities leave the function to their counties.

Streets and Sidewalks

State government has responsibility for constructing and maintaining all public roads outside cities. Inside its boundaries, a city shares in road construction and maintenance responsibilities, on the basis of an agreement between the city and the State Department of Transportation. In general, the state retains responsibility for city streets that carry traffic through the city or to major destinations within the city, such as government buildings, industrial plants, shopping centers, and the like. All other city streets are the city's responsibility. (For most city functions, state law authorizes cities to perform the function outside the city as well as within. That is not true, however, with streets and sidewalks; cities may spend money on these activities only within city limits.)

Cities meet their street-related costs from a variety of sources. First, the state shares a portion of its motor fuels taxes with cities, the so-called "Powell Bill" funds. Second, cities may use local taxes and other general revenues to supplement the state aid. Third, many cities help finance street construction or major improvements through special, or benefit, assessments, under which owners of property that abuts the improved or new street pay part or all of the cost. Finally, the typical subdivision control ordinance requires, as a condition of city approval of a subdivision, that the developer construct streets within the subdivision to city standards; once completed, the streets are dedicated to the city.

Sidewalks within a city are normally entirely the responsibility of the city, even on roads maintained by the state. Cities finance sidewalks in much the same way they finance streets, including with Powell Bill funds.

Public Enterprises

Cities operate a variety of public enterprises—services that are or easily can be fully or largely financed by charges to those who use them. The list includes those services normally considered to be public utilities, as well as a few others. Each of these services is often provided by private enterprise rather than by city government. Although an identifying characteristic of enterprise services is their capacity to be fully supported by charges to users, state law does not require that they be fully self-supporting, and a city may properly use local tax revenues to supplement or supplant user-charge revenues. As a practical matter, though, except for solid-waste collection services, cities normally finance their public enterprises with user charges whenever possible, relying on tax revenues only when charges prove insufficient. None of the enterprises operated by cities is subject to the rate-making supervision of the state's Utilities Commission; the city governing board enjoys complete authority to set rates and charges.

The principal city-operated enterprises are set out below.

Water and Sewerage Services

Community water and sewerage systems are probably the enterprises most commonly operated by North Carolina cities. Normally, charges to customers fully finance operations, including the cost of repaying any debt incurred in constructing the facilities. Water and sewer line extensions are often financed in the same manner as are street improvements:

by special assessments or by requiring that lines be built and dedicated by subdivision developers.

State law also defines stormwater regulation as a city enterprise, mainly to facilitate paying for federally required stormwater measures by charges against water or sewerage system customers.

Electricity and Gas

Seventy-odd North Carolina cities operate electrical distribution systems, and a handful of these also distribute natural gas. Many of these systems serve not only the residents of the city but also large areas outside the city. Electricity and gas systems normally are fully supported by charges to users and sometimes contribute to the support of other city services and functions as well.

Solid-Waste Collection and Disposal

Solid-waste collection is commonly a city-provided service in North Carolina, most often through city employees but sometimes by city contract with one or more private collectors. This service differs from the other enterprises in that cities traditionally finance it from local tax revenues rather than from direct charges to users of the service. Disposal of solid wastes, on the other hand, has moved far toward being primarily a county function in North Carolina. So, while cities continue to collect solid wastes, they now most often dispose of those wastes in county-operated (or privately-operated) landfills.

Parking

Many cities provide off-street parking facilities, particularly in their central business districts. On-street parking is more a part of the city's traffic control system than an enterprise, even though some revenues are realized from meters.

Public Transportation

Some sort of bus system operates in most North Carolina cities with populations exceeding 25,000, and usually that system is city-owned. (In addition, Charlotte owns and operates a light rail system partially funded by a specially authorized local sales and use tax.) City bus systems are usually partly supported from local tax revenues and federal grant funds, inasmuch as fares do not meet all costs.

Airports

A few cities in North Carolina operate airports, although this is increasingly a county or even regional function. Perhaps two or three of the largest airports in the state are fully self-supporting from landing fees, property rentals, and other charges, but most airports require some subsidy from local tax revenues.

Cemeteries

Many cities operate cemeteries, supporting them through a combination of fees, charges, and tax revenues.

Cable Television and Related Communications Services

A very small group of cities provide cable television and related communications services (such as high-speed internet access) as a city enterprise. Legislation enacted in 2011, however, seeks to discourage other cities from joining this small group by requiring that all city costs for the service be met by system revenues and by requiring voter approval before any debt of any kind can be incurred to construct the system.

Auditoriums, Coliseums, Convention Centers

Most of North Carolina's larger cities— those with populations over 50,000—operate one or more of these types of facilities. Frequently the governing board appoints a special commission to operate the facilities, which require some subsidy (at least to pay debt charges on the funds borrowed to build them) from local tax revenues.

Leisure and Cultural Activities

Parks and Recreation

Cities offer or support recreation programs in a variety of ways. One city might own one or more parks and playgrounds that permit largely unsupervised play. Another might supplement this with a summer or year-round recreation program—for children, older citizens, or everyone. Still another city might simply contribute a small amount to a private program—for example, a privately sponsored basketball league—expecting it to provide recreation opportunities for the city's residents. In planning and operating recreation programs, cities frequently rely extensively on recreation boards or commissions, composed of citizens appointed by the governing board. Although a few recreation programs and facilities might return some revenues (such as tennis courts, a golf course, or a bridge class), most financial support comes from local taxes and other general revenues.

Libraries

Although originally a city function, libraries have, partly from state government initiative, become primarily a county responsibility. But cities are still authorized to operate or support library systems, and so a few retain their own libraries while others contribute to the support of a county library.

Cultural Affairs

Cities may, and in various ways do, support cultural activities such as museums, festivals, musical groups, and so on. Support in this area comes primarily in the form of contributions, and the amounts of money involved are not large.

Housing and Development

Housing and Community Development

Stimulated by the availability of federal assistance, and with programs largely shaped by the conditions of that assistance, cities and city agencies have been actively concerned since the 1930s with eliminating urban blight and providing decent housing for the poor. The original federal program addressing these issues, beginning in the 1930s and continuing today, encouraged the construction of public housing for the poor and the elderly, under the management of housing authorities created by but largely independent of city governing boards. Although the details of housing programs have evolved over time, housing authorities continue to provide and manage public housing.

The next great federal initiative, from the late 1940s and early 1950s, was urban renewal, managed in North Carolina by redevelopment commissions—agencies much like housing authorities in their relationship to their parent cities. Classic urban renewal involved the purchasing and clearing of blighted areas by the redevelopment commission, then the conveyance of parcels of the cleared land to public or institutional users or to private developers. Urban renewal, as a separate federal program, ended with the enactment of the federal community development program in the 1970s, and there are very few redevelopment commissions remaining in North Carolina.

Community development seeks, broadly, to improve the living environment of the poor by such means as assisting in the rehabilitation of decaying private housing and improving public facilities, such as streets or parks, in low or moderate income neighborhoods. Community development differs from its predecessor programs in taking a broader view of suitable redevelopment activities and by giving the local governments that receive federal support greater flexibility in devising the content and structure of their community development programs.

A related program that has been largely locally financed is housing code enforcement. Housing codes seek to maintain existing structures in livable conditions; if a house fails to meet code standards, a city may order it repaired or, in extreme cases, torn down.

Economic Development

Cities may undertake a variety of programs that seek to improve economic and business conditions within and near their borders. These programs include the recruitment of new industry, support of existing businesses, downtown revitalization, and worker training programs.

Regulation of Development

Land Use Regulation

Cities in North Carolina enjoy broad authority to plan for and regulate the uses and development of land within the city and, to some extent, in the area immediately outside the city. In developing the city's basic comprehensive plan, a document with no binding force but intended to guide later city actions, the governing board is normally advised by a citizen planning commission. The plan itself, once completed, may be implemented both through direct city action and through city regulation of private action. The plan ought to guide the city as it acquires and constructs public facilities, such as street and utility systems extensions and park land. It also should shape the principal regulatory tools available for its implementation—the zoning ordinance and the subdivision control ordinance. (Many cities combine these two ordinances, and other development regulations, into a single unified development ordinance.)

A zoning ordinance divides a city into a series of districts (zones) and specifies what land uses are proper within each district. A subdivision control ordinance, as its name suggests, specifies minimum standards that any new subdivision must meet, such as aligning new streets with existing and planned ones or assuring that storm drainage facilities are sufficient. It also typically requires the construction of some public improvements—such as streets, water and sewer lines, and perhaps playgrounds—that will be turned over to the city when complete. A good part of any city governing board's time is devoted to the amendment and administration of zoning and subdivision ordinances.

Once new construction begins, it must comply with the state building code, which cities enforce (or contract with third parties to enforce) within their planning jurisdictions. North Carolina operates under a statewide building code rather than local codes adopted by each city and county.

Historic Preservation and Aesthetics

North Carolina law permits cities to undertake a variety of activities in support of historic preservation. Cities may financially support local preservation organizations. They may designate suitable areas within their limits as historic districts or designate individual buildings and structures as historic properties; these steps impose special regulations on individual properties within an historic district or on designated historic properties. A city that designates either historic districts or properties must appoint an historic preservation commission to administer the relevant ordinances.

In the broader area of aesthetics, cities may take such actions as establishing an appearance commission to advise on the appearance of major new public and private construction within the city's planning jurisdiction, adopt sign control ordinances, and buy property to be preserved as open space.

Administrative Functions

To offer the services and establish and enforce the regulations that directly affect citizens, a city must provide various administrative services to itself, including central management, financial management, purchasing, revenue collection, human resources, record-keeping, and the like.[1] In a very small town, each of these tasks might be performed by the same person, the town clerk. As a city grows, the administrative burdens grow, and several officials might be appointed to handle them. A large city is likely to place the functions mentioned above under the charge of a manager and perhaps one or more deputy or assistant managers, a budget director, a finance director, a purchasing agent, a revenue collector, a human resources director, and the city clerk. In addition, each city must have an attorney, who is appointed by the governing board and serves at that entity's pleasure. Many of the larger

---

1. The overwhelming majority of North Carolina cities have contracted with their counties for the latter to collect the cities' property taxes, though many cities collect other taxes through their own employees.

cities employ one or more attorneys full time, but most cities retain an attorney in private practice to serve as city attorney.

County Functions

The preceding section omits a number of functions associated with local government in North Carolina; these functions are excluded because they are the sole responsibility of county—as opposed to city—government. The register of deeds, who registers and files deeds and other legal instruments, is a county official. So is the sheriff, who not only provides law enforcement outside of cities but also operates the jail, serves process, and provides court-support services. North Carolina's court system is largely state-operated and state-funded, but counties are responsible for providing local court facilities and meeting certain costs of the court system. Public health and mental health are the primary legal responsibility of counties, while hospital services have become, in fact, a county function. State law requires counties to provide a broad range of social services and contains no general authorization to cities to do so. And finally, and perhaps most confusingly, public education is, at the local level, a county responsibility.

The important point to remember about cities and schools is that city government in North Carolina has almost no official role in the public school system. The local financial responsibility for public education is the county's, for both county and city school administrative units. Despite their names, city school administrative units, with minor exceptions, have no relationship to city government. They are characterized as city units simply to differentiate them from the county school administrative unit (which has no supervisory control over them), and their borders only rarely match city borders. (Minor exceptions to the roles and responsibilities discussed here are the (very) few city school boards that are appointed by the city government's governing board and the (very) few city governing boards that levy supplemental school taxes on behalf of the city school unit.) Cities must often work with school boards, of course, in coordinating school sites with city development plans, in providing recreation, and so on, but these situations involve relationships between two separate public bodies, not between a city and one of its agencies.

Financing City Government

Probably the single most important task that a city council undertakes each year is adopting the city's annual budget ordinance. Through that ordinance the council decides what services the city will provide its citizens, the extent of each service, and how those services will be paid for. The sections below briefly describe the budget process, the revenues available to a city to finance city government, and the ways by which a city may borrow money for capital projects.

Budgeting

North Carolina cities operate under a July 1–June 30 fiscal year. During that period, most city expenditures are made pursuant to an annual budget ordinance adopted by the council. This ordinance, adopted around the beginning of the fiscal year, serves to authorize city expenditures, assure that expenditures and revenues are in balance, and levy property taxes for that year. A council may also adopt project ordinances to authorize expenditures on capital projects or on operations funded by a federal or state grant. A city's administration is bound by the expenditure authorizations of the budget ordinance and any project ordinances. Those authorizations may not be exceeded, nor may moneys be spent for a purpose for which there is no authorization.

Revenues

North Carolina cities finance their operations from a variety of revenues—local taxes, fees and charges, state-shared taxes, and federal and state grants. Although cities enjoy a good deal of flexibility in determining which revenues to use and how much reliance to place on each source, a pattern does exist. The primary local revenue sources are the property tax and user charges for major municipal utility services—water, sewer, electricity, and gas. Other major revenue sources are the local-option sales tax and various state-shared taxes; for larger cities, federal grants can also be important funding sources. There are other revenue sources that, while of minor impact individually, can be significant when added together. Examples include ABC store revenues, investment income, and, particularly with larger cities, regulatory fees.

Local Taxes

Cities, as creatures of the North Carolina General Assembly, may levy only those taxes specifically authorized by that legislative body, the most important of which—by far—is the property tax. In addition, cities share in the proceeds of the local-option sales and use tax, which is levied by the board of county commissioners.

Property taxes—which are levied on both real and personal property—are the single most important source of tax revenue to cities, and in many cities the most important source of revenue of any sort. In the great majority of cities, the only role the city has in property tax administration is to levy the tax; cities are also permitted to collect property taxes, but most contract with their counties to do so on their behalf. The property tax base is defined by the General Assembly, because only the General Assembly may exempt property from taxation or classify it for tax purposes. Once within the base, property is appraised for taxation by the county tax assessor and, for certain limited classes of property, by the State Department of Revenue, and a city must accept those valuations.

The second most important tax source for cities is the local-option sales and use tax. This tax was first authorized in 1971 and has been modified and increased several times in the years since. Currently, all counties in North Carolina levy a 2 percent local-option sales and use tax, and a handful levy an additional 0.25 percent, through approval by the county's voters. (Mecklenburg County levies an additional .50 percent, through local legislation and voter approval.) A portion of the proceeds from this tax is distributed to each city and town in the county. The criterion for distribution—selected by the county's board of commissioners—is either population (with all county citizens being counted for the county) or the size of each unit's property tax levy. Cities may use sales and use tax revenues for any city government function or activity.

Cities may also levy five other relatively minor types of taxes under state law. First, a city may levy privilege license taxes for the privilege of carrying on a business or engaging in an occupation, trade, or profession within the city. Second, a city may levy a tax on the privilege of keeping "any domestic animal, including dogs and cats." Despite the statutory invitation to tax cats and other pets, in practice the tax is almost universally limited to dogs. Third, each city may place a license tax on each motor vehicle "resident" within the city. The general law rate is $5 per vehicle (plus another possible $5 if the city operates a public transportation system), but a number of cities have local act authority to impose somewhat higher vehicle taxes. Finally cities may levy gross receipts taxes on rental car operations within the city and on the rental of heavy equipment within the city.

State-Shared Taxes

A portion of the proceeds of a number of state-levied taxes are shared with cities; as a group these are characterized as state-shared taxes.

The state levies three taxes that emerged from its long-time practice of taxing the franchises of public utilities, although the form of some of the taxes has changed over time. First, the state levies a franchise tax on electric power companies and shares with each city a portion of the tax based on sales of electricity within that city. Second, the state levies a sales tax on the gross receipts of telecommunications services and shares a portion of the proceeds with each city based on a detailed statutory formula. Finally, the state levies an excise tax on the distribution of piped natural gas and shares half the proceeds with each city within which such gas is sold.

The state levies a variety of liquor taxes. These include excise taxes on beer and wine, and a portion of the proceeds of these taxes is shared with each city (and county) within which those beverages may legally be sold. The distribution is based upon population.

The state levies a tax on motor fuels and a tax on the sale of motor vehicles and shares a portion of the proceeds with cities. (This is the so-called Powell Bill money.) Three-quarters of the amount available for cities is distributed based on each city's population, and the remaining funds are distributed based on the number of miles of city-maintained streets within each city. Unlike the state-shared revenues described above, these moneys are earmarked and may be used only for street- and sidewalk-related expenditures.

Each of the three remaining state-shared taxes earmarks some or all of the proceeds for distribution to cities. First, the video programming services tax was levied when the state assumed exclusive franchising authority for cable television and related services, and a portion of the tax proceeds is shared with cities as a replacement for the local franchise taxes that cities levied on cable systems. Cities must use a portion of these moneys to support their local public educational or public access channels. Second, the state levies a statewide excise tax on the disposal of solid waste and shares a portion of the revenues with counties and cities that provide solid-waste management services; the proceeds distributed to local governments must be used for those solid-waste management services. Third, the state's 911 Board levies a charge on telephone subscribers and distributes a portion of the proceeds to local governments operating 911 systems; the proceeds must be used to fund those systems.

Other Local Revenues

Cities may also levy a variety of fees and charges, some quite important, others quite small. The section on public enterprises, above, indicated that cities may and do levy charges for those types of services and facilities; several of these, particularly water and sewer charges, normally fully support the enterprise involved, while electric and gas revenues sometimes are large enough to support other functions as well. Among the other sorts of revenue sources that a city may use are special assessments, which are levied against properties that received special benefits from new or improved streets or sidewalks or extended water or sewer lines; profits from alcoholic beverage control stores; permit fees; and investment income.

Borrowed Funds

Cities borrow money by issuing bonds, notes, or other securities that evidence the underlying debt. They do so within a constitutional and statutory framework that establishes several basic policies. First, with only minor exceptions, cities may borrow money only to acquire or construct capital assets. They may not balance their budgets with borrowed funds, thereby imposing the cost of current operations on future taxpayers. The principal exception to this rule permits local governments to borrow in anticipation of receiving current revenues, but anticipation debt (which is, in any event, rarely used in North Carolina) must be repaid when those current revenues are in fact collected.

Second, local government borrowing is subject to an unusual degree of state supervision. When a city wishes to borrow, in most instances a state agency, the Local Government Commission (LGC), must first approve the proposed borrowing and then sell the bonds, notes, or other securities on behalf of the local government. The LGC was established in 1931, primarily to help local governments solve their fiscal problems in the Great Depression. Since then, one of its principal tasks has been to assure that local governments do not borrow money they do not have the financial strength to repay. The LGC's success in that function has given North Carolina local governments' securities an outstanding national reputation.

Third, the North Carolina General Statutes authorize local governments to use a variety of forms of borrowing, which fundamentally differ according to the nature of the security—the repayment promise—given by the local government to the holders of its debt. These are the forms of security currently available to cities and other local governments in the state:

- The local government's power to levy taxes (General obligation bonds).
- The capital asset that the local government will build or buy with the borrowed funds (Installment financings and Certificates of Participation (COPs)).
- The net revenues generated by the facility or system constructed or improved with the borrowed funds (Revenue bonds).
- Revenues other than locally levied taxes (Special obligation bonds, which may be issued for only a limited number of purposes).
- Taxes on the increase in private property values caused by the construction or improvements financed with the borrowed funds (Project development bonds, also known as tax increment bonds).

Finally, the North Carolina Constitution requires that most general obligation debt—debt that is secured by the local government's power and promise to levy taxes—be approved by the voters of the borrowing local government before the debt may be issued. (Voter approval is not required for other forms of debt.)

PART 2
The Mayor and Council

5   Organizing the Council

A city council, like the city it serves, has a continuing, perpetual existence.[1] Even though its members may change, the council continues on unaffected. Thus, a proceeding (such as a condemnation) that is begun before an election may be continued and completed after the election, even though the membership of the council has changed. Despite their continuing existence, all city councils must reorganize themselves after each city election. This chapter reviews the council's reorganization process.

Timing

The usual time for city council organizational meetings is the council's first regular meeting in December following each city election. Section 160A-68 of the North Carolina General Statutes (hereinafter G.S.), however, permits the outgoing council to schedule an earlier time for the organizational meeting if it so wishes. (The incoming council has no authority to move the organizational meeting if the outgoing council is unwilling to do so.) The council may schedule this earlier meeting for any time during the period that begins with the day the election results are officially determined and published and that ends with the day of the council's first regular meeting in December. In the absence of any action by the outgoing council, the organizational meeting is held at that first December meeting.

If a newly elected council member cannot attend the organizational meeting, he or she may take the oath of office at any convenient time after the organizational meeting. Unless a person has been reelected and is continuing in office, the statutes do not appear to permit someone to be sworn into office (thereby dislodging the incumbent) until the organizational meeting.

---

1. Pegram v. Comm'rs of Cleveland Cnty., 65 N.C. 114 (1871).

Order of Business

The common practice at organizational meetings is for the outgoing council to complete any old business and then recognize members who are retiring from council service. The outgoing mayor presides over this portion of the council meeting. The newly elected members are then sworn in, and, under the direction of the incoming mayor, the new council commences its work.

Qualifying for Office

Elected officials in North Carolina qualify for the office to which they have been elected by taking and subscribing (that is, signing) the oath set out in article VI, section 7, of the state constitution. The oath reads:

> I, . . . , do solemnly swear (or affirm) that I will support and maintain the Constitution and laws of the United States, and the Constitution and laws of North Carolina not inconsistent therewith, and that I will faithfully discharge the duties of my office as . . . , so help me God.

If a city's charter sets out a council oath different from the constitutional oath above, new council members should take both oaths. G.S. 160A-61 directs that when the oath (or oaths) is taken and signed, it is to be filed with the city clerk.

G.S. 11-7.1 lists the officers qualified to administer oaths: active or retired North Carolina justices or judges; members of the federal judiciary; magistrates; clerks, deputy clerks, and assistant clerks of superior court; the North Carolina Secretary of State; notaries public; registers of deeds; mayors; chairs of the board of county commissioners; members of the North Carolina General Assembly; city clerks; and clerks to county boards of commissioners. Choosing the person to swear in a newly elected council is usually a matter of tradition: one city will ask a local judge, another, the clerk of superior court, and a third, the outgoing mayor or the city clerk.

Electing Officers

Besides taking the oath, the only action the council is obliged to take at the organizational meeting is to elect the mayor pro tempore ("pro tem") (and, in cities in which the council elects the mayor, the mayor). G.S. 160A-71 directs that each council elect a mayor pro tem at the organizational meeting. In a very few cities, the city charter directs some different method of selecting the mayor pro tem—for example, by giving the appointment to the mayor or by designating the leading vote-getter for council as mayor pro tem. (The duties of the mayor pro tem are discussed in Chapter 6, below.)

Other Actions

Although taking the oath of office and electing the mayor pro tem (and mayor, if appropriate) are the only actions that must be taken at the organizational meeting, many councils by tradition take other actions as well. They may, for example, reappoint (or perhaps dismiss) persons who hold positions at the pleasure of the council—the manager, the attorney, or the clerk. Or they may fill committee positions or readopt the meeting schedule.

None of these traditional actions is necessary. Because the council is a continuing body, the outgoing council's appointment of officers or establishment of meeting times remains effective with the new council and need not be reaffirmed. Only if a change is intended is action necessary, and even then it need not come at the organizational meeting.

6 City Officers

This chapter discusses the offices of mayor and mayor pro tem and the procedures for filling vacancies on the council and in the office of mayor.

The Mayor

Chapter 3 describes in a general way the powers and role of the mayor in North Carolina cities. As noted in that description, a mayor has formal legal powers. Under the general law, he or she presides over council meetings and may vote only to break a tie. The mayor may call special meetings of the council, administer oaths, and occasionally make various appointments. Finally, the mayor is recognized as the head of city government for ceremonial purposes and for receiving service of legal papers. In many cities the mayor signs all contracts on behalf of the city, but unless the city's charter gives the mayor that responsibility, the practice is rooted more in tradition than in law.

The Mayor Pro Tempore

Section 160A-70 of the North Carolina General Statutes (hereinafter G.S.) directs that each city council, at its organizational meeting, elect a mayor pro tempore, who is to serve at its pleasure. (Some city charters set a specific term for the pro tem, usually two years.) The direct role of the mayor pro tem is to preside over council meetings in the mayor's absence. While presiding, the mayor pro tem may vote as a council member but may not as presiding officer vote to break any tie he or she helped to create. (In the absence of both officials, the council members who are present at a meeting may select a temporary presiding officer.)

Although there is a widespread belief that a mayor pro tem automatically assumes all of the mayor's duties in the latter's absence or disability, the general law actually appears to require some further council action. G.S. 160A-70 states that in the mayor's absence the council may confer any mayoral power or duty on the mayor pro tem. The language of the statute implies, first, that some council action is necessary, and, second, that the council may pick and choose which duties to transfer to the mayor pro tem.

The council must also act if the mayor becomes disabled—for example, by suffering a stroke. Under G.S. 160A-70, the council may declare, by unanimous vote only, the mayor to be disabled and then confer any of the mayor's duties on the mayor pro tem. A mayor declared disabled may resume his or her duties by declaring that he or she is fit and by receiving the concurrence of a majority of the council's members.

Council and Mayoral Vacancies

Occasionally a vacancy occurs in a council seat or the mayor's office—usually by resignation or death, infrequently by action of law, as when a council member simply moves away without formally resigning.[1] One unanswered question under North Carolina law is whether a resignation becomes effective when made or only when it is accepted by the council.[2] Requiring acceptance does not mean that a person cannot resign in the absence of acceptance; rather, it means that he or she may withdraw the resignation at any time before acceptance.

The council fills a vacancy by appointing a replacement member. If the person leaving office was serving a two-year term or was in or near the last half of a four-year term, the appointee serves for the remainder of the unexpired term. If the person leaving office was in the first two years of a four-year term, however, and the vacancy occurs more than ninety days before the next city election, the appointee serves only until the organizational meeting following that election; voters will select a candidate to fill the last two years of the term.

In general, a council has great freedom in filling a vacancy, regarding both the procedures it follows and the person it appoints. Some councils depend on council members to

---

1. Sometimes a council member moves out of the city but, despite the statement in G.S. 160A-59 that such an action causes his or her seat to become ipso facto vacant, continues to attend and participate in council meetings. In such a situation, it may be open to the council, after notice to the member and a hearing into the facts, to determine whether he or she has moved from the city and then, if appropriate, to declare the seat vacant and proceed to fill it. Alternatively, the council might report the facts to the local board of elections, which has the power to determine if a person has moved from the city and thereby lost his or her eligibility to vote in city elections. A person who cannot vote in city elections in not eligible to serve on the council.

2. This issue is discussed in David M. Lawrence, *Must a Public Official's Resignation Be Accepted in Order to Be Effective?* POPULAR GOVERNMENT 38–39 (UNC Institute of Government, Spring 1985).

locate candidates for filling the vacancy; others require that interested citizens file a formal application. The person appointed to the vacancy must be qualified to run for and hold the office—that is, the person must be a registered voter resident in the city and, if appropriate, in the proper council district; if city elections are partisan, the person also must be of the same party as the person who vacated the seat.[3] Those are the only requirements, however, of the general law. Any other constraints, such as automatically appointing the top vote-getter among the unsuccessful candidates in the last city election or acting on advice from the local executive committee of the political party to which the person vacating the seat belonged, are purely voluntary.

---

3. *See* G.S. 160A-63.

7   Council Meetings

Chapter 3 made the point—worth repeating as we begin the discussion of council meetings—that a city council is a collegial body that may act only when properly convened in a legal meeting. One member may not act on behalf of the entire group (unless it has properly authorized the member to do so), nor may the entire group act as a city council at an informal gathering that was not called according to law.[1] Thus it is important to be familiar with the requirements for regular, special, and recessed meetings.

Regular Meetings

Section 160A-71 of the North Carolina General Statutes (hereinafter G.S.) charges each city council to fix the time and place of its regular meetings. (If a council fails to act, the statute directs that meetings be held on the first Monday of each month at 10 a.m.) The general law places no requirement or limitations of frequency or time of day on regular meetings, although some city charters do require that there be at least one, or occasionally two or more, a month.

If a council's regular meeting date falls on a holiday, how should that meeting be rescheduled? The most convenient way is to provide for such a contingency in the ordinance that establishes the regular meeting schedule. For example, the ordinance might state that whenever a council meeting falls on a public holiday (and these might be listed), the meeting is automatically rescheduled for the next day. In the absence of such a provision, a meeting rescheduled because of a holiday is a special meeting and must be called in the manner required for special meetings.

G.S. 143-318.12, the state open meetings law, requires that the council's schedule of regular meetings be filed with the city clerk and that any changes in the schedule be filed at least

---

1. Town of Bath v. Norman, 226 N.C. 502, 39 S.E.2d 363 (1946); London v. Comm'rs for Yancey Cnty., 193 N.C. 100, 136 S.E.346 (1927).

seven days before the day of the first meeting under the changed schedule. In addition, if the city maintains a website, it must post the regular meeting schedule on that site. These filings constitute the only public notice required for regular meetings.

Canceling a Meeting

Sometimes, before a scheduled meeting is held, it becomes clear that a quorum of the council will not be able to attend, and therefore no legal meeting will be possible. As a consequence, city officials decide to cancel the meeting. Unfortunately, there is no statutory procedure for doing so. Rather, what has worked best in practice is for the mayor, manager, or clerk to notify the entire council that the meeting is canceled, to post a notice to that effect on the council's bulletin board and the city's webpage, and to notify the news media of the cancellation in hopes they will be able to get the word out to citizens.

Special Meetings

Special meetings may be called or held in any of three ways. First, the council may antici-pate the need for the meeting and schedule it during any regular meeting or duly called special meeting. Second, the mayor, the mayor pro tem, or any two members of the council may call a special meeting.[2] This is done by preparing and signing a written notice of the meeting, which sets out its time, its place, and the subjects to be considered, and by having this notice delivered to each council member or each member's home. Under G.S. 160A-71, this notice must be delivered at least six hours before the meeting, but the open meetings law requires forty-eight hours' public notice of a special meeting (see the discussion at the end of this section). Third, a special meeting may be held whenever the entire member-ship of the council is together or when the absent members have signed a waiver. Because the public notice required by the open meetings law must still be given for such a special meeting, the only practical use of this provision is when the notice given under the second method is defective or when there is an emergency and the council cannot wait even for six hours' notice to council members.

In general, a council may take any action at a special meeting that it could take at a regu-lar meeting, but a few exceptions do exist. For example, ordinances awarding or amending

---

2. Some city charters require a majority of council members to call for a special meeting or permit the mayor pro tempore to act only in the mayor's absence. Such a charter provision supersedes the general law provisions described in the text.

franchises must be adopted at regular meetings, and several procedures for selling property require that action be taken at regular meetings. (Even so, a council may discuss these matters at a special meeting; it simply may not act on them.) Because of these exceptions, a council should consult its attorney before taking any action at a special meeting to ascertain what actions may properly be taken at that meeting.

In addition, the manner in which a special meeting is called can limit the subjects that may be discussed at the meeting. Any item appropriate for a special meeting may be discussed or acted on during a meeting that was scheduled at an earlier council meeting. But if the meeting is held pursuant to a special call, its subject matter may be further limited. The call itself is required to specify the "subjects to be considered" at the meeting. Unless the entire council is present or those absent have signed a waiver, only the items of business listed in the call may be transacted. The purpose of this limitation is to protect absent council members, and action taken in violation of the limitation is probably void.[3] On occasion, some councils have attempted to make a gesture toward this protective purpose and still leave themselves free to act on other matters during a called meeting by including in the call, as a final item of business, some variant of the phrase "any other matter to come before the board." In at least one instance, a court in another state has held that action taken at a special meeting pursuant to that kind of blanket subject-matter listing was invalid.[4]

The open meetings law establishes additional procedures that must be followed for each special meeting of a council, no matter how called. G.S. 143-318.12 requires forty-eight hours' public notice of any special meeting (except an emergency meeting). The notice—which includes the time, place, and purpose of the meeting—must be posted on the council's principal bulletin board and on the city's website. The notice also must be mailed, emailed, or delivered (not telephoned) to anyone who has made a written request for notice. If an emergency requiring "the immediate consideration" of the council demands that a council meet more quickly than within forty-eight hours, the open meetings law directs that public notice be given to any local news medium that has made a written request for such notice. No other public notice is required for an emergency meeting.

---

3. *See, e.g.,* Miss. State Bd. of Educ. v. Noble, 388 So. 2d 488 (Miss. 1980); Haworth Bd. of Educ. v. Havens, 637 P.2d 902 (Okla. Civ. App. 1981).

4. Mills v. City of San Antonio, 65 S.W.2d 1121 (Tex. App. 1901).

Recessed Meetings

If a city council cannot finish the business on its agenda at a particular meeting, it may wish to recess the meeting and return later that same evening or a few days later to finish the agenda. When the recess specifies a "time certain"—that is, a specific date and time for continuing—the later meeting is considered to be a "recessed session" of the original meeting.[5] Instead of "recessing to a time certain," a council may simply call a special meeting to conclude its business. There are, however, at least two advantages to recessing to a time certain. First, a recessed meeting is considered to be a continuation of the original meeting; thus, if the original meeting was a regular meeting, so is the recessed meeting. If the subject to be considered is one of those that may be acted on only at a regular meeting, a recessed session will allow for action. Second, the special-meeting notice rules of the open meetings law do not extend to recessed meetings. Thus, if proper notice was given of the original meeting and the motion to recess was adopted in open session at the original meeting, no further public notice is required for the recessed session.

Adjournment

To adjourn a meeting of a city council, a majority of the council members must vote for a motion to adjourn. While a mayor or other presiding officer probably has the power to unilaterally declare a short recess, particularly to give heightened emotions a chance to calm down, he or she has no power to unilaterally declare that a meeting be adjourned.

---

5. If a council recesses or adjourns subject to call of its presiding officer, it is not considered to be recessing to a time certain, and the subsequent meeting is simply a special meeting. Village of Loon Valley v. Spellum, 208 N.W.2d 916 (Wis. 1926).

8 Council Action

This chapter discusses the prerequisites to and the procedures for council action. In general, a council acts by ordinance, by resolution, or by motion (or order). No North Carolina statute or case defines these terms, so no definitive distinctions can be drawn among these classes of action. A few points can be suggested, however.

First, it often matters very little whether an action is taken by ordinance, resolution, or motion.[1] In many states, ordinances—but not other actions—may be adopted only after a public hearing, must be published once adopted, do not take effect for a given number of days after adoption, or are subject to referendum (that is, veto by the voters). North Carolina general law contains none of these requirements, although such requirements occasionally appear in city charters. About the only statutory attribute that an ordinance bears in this state is that it needs a larger majority for adoption than do other actions. Therefore, if an action is adopted by a vote sufficient to pass an ordinance, it is unlikely that a court would invalidate the action simply because it was incorrectly labeled a "resolution" or "motion."

Second, if the distinction becomes important, textbooks usually define an ordinance as a permanent rule of conduct imposed by a city on its citizens. Thus, ordinances may limit the noise a person may make, regulate how a person may use his or her land, or require a business to treat its sewage before emptying it into the city's water system. In addition, North Carolina statutes normally characterize as ordinances those actions by which a city levies taxes or appropriates money.

Third, whether an action is a resolution or a motion is often more a matter of tradition than of law. Many city councils authorize contracts, deeds, or lawsuits, establish committees, or grant individual licenses by resolution; others take these actions by motion. No

---

1. *But see* Howell v. Town of Carolina Beach, 106 N.C. App. 410, 417 S.E.2d 277 (1992).

The North Carolina Court of Appeals, following the lead of the federal Fourth Circuit Court of Appeals, has distinguished between local government personnel policies that are adopted by *ordinance* and those that are adopted by *resolution*. The former, but not the latter, may have the effect of creating for local government employees property rights in their employment.

effect comes from this choice under the general law, and so normally a council is free to proceed with either form of action.

Quorum

As noted earlier, a council may not act unless it does so during a legally constituted meeting, and a meeting is not legally constituted unless a quorum is present. G.S. 160A-74 defines a quorum as a majority of the actual membership of the council, including the mayor, but not including vacant seats. For example, if a city is governed by a five-member council plus the mayor, the actual membership of the group is six, and thus the quorum is any four of the six. But if one seat is vacant, the membership becomes five, and the quorum, three.

Some states follow a doctrine that further affects whether a quorum is present. If a person is disqualified to vote on a subject—for example, because of a potential conflict of interest—he or she may not be counted as present for quorum purposes when that subject is discussed. Although neither the North Carolina statutes nor any North Carolina appellate case has addressed this question, McQuillin's treatise on city government suggests that this doctrine is the general rule around the country.[2]

Once a quorum has been obtained and the meeting convened, a council member may not destroy the quorum by simply getting up and leaving. G.S. 160A-74 provides that if a member withdraws from the meeting without being excused by a majority vote of the remaining members present, he or she is still counted as present for purposes of a quorum. Indeed, the law stipulates that the absent member continues to vote after he or she is gone. (See the discussion of unexcused abstentions on page 50 for an explanation of this phenomenon.) This rule applies only to a member who has been at a meeting and then leaves, not to a member who never showed up at all.

Voting Rules

The number of council members who must vote in favor of a measure for that measure to pass depends upon a number of factors: whether the measure is an ordinance or some other form of action, and if an ordinance, what kind; when the measure first came before the council; and whether any members have been excused from voting on the measure.

---

2. 4 McQuillin, A Treatise on the Law of Municipal Corporations § 13.35a (3d ed. 1978).

Ordinances

Day of Introduction

To be adopted on the day it is introduced, an ordinance, or any action that has the effect of an ordinance, must be approved by a vote of at least two-thirds of the actual council membership, excluding vacant seats. In determining the membership, the mayor is not counted unless he or she has the right to vote on all questions before the council. Thus, if a council has seven members and is presided over by a mayor who votes only to break ties, five members must vote in favor of an ordinance if that ordinance is to be adopted on the day it is first introduced. But if there is a vacant seat, the actual membership is six, and only four votes are required to adopt the ordinance that first day. Table 8.1, below, sets out the required two-thirds (and majority) vote in the variously-sized city councils in North Carolina.

In general, one of four consequences might result from council consideration of an ordinance on the day it is introduced. First, the council might consider and vote on the ordinance, and a majority of those present might vote against it. In that case, the measure is defeated, and if it is again brought before the council, it is considered a new introduction. Second, the council might give the measure the requisite two-thirds vote, thereby adopting it. Third, the council might pass the measure, but not by a two-thirds majority. In that case, the measure is neither adopted nor defeated; it needs only the approval of a regular majority (defined in the section entitled "The General Rule," below) at a later meeting to be adopted. Fourth, the proposal might be discussed but not voted on. The result then is the same as in the third situation: the measure may be adopted by a regular majority at a later meeting.

What constitutes the "day of introduction" of an ordinance? G.S. 160A-75 specifies that the day of introduction is the day the council first votes on the subject matter of the ordinance. This statutory elaboration is not entirely clear, but the purpose of the rule seems to be to prevent a council from quickly bringing up and adopting an ordinance before the entire council or the public has a chance to react—unless the ordinance has the support of at least two-thirds of the members. If this is a correct understanding of the rule's purpose, it would be served by any vote in the council that involves the ordinance or its subject matter and that gives notice that the council is considering the ordinance's adoption. For example, each of the following actions serves these apparent purposes and therefore ought to qualify as a "day-of-introduction" vote:

- a discussion of the ordinance, followed by a vote to refer it to committee;
- voting to schedule a public hearing on the ordinance;

- voting to direct the city's administration to prepare an ordinance on a specific subject; and, of course,
- voting on whether to adopt the ordinance.

Indeed, it is not clear that any vote is or ought to be required to meet the "introduction" definition. If a council brings up and discusses a proposed ordinance at length, then simply agrees with the mayor's suggestion to take the matter up again at a later meeting, that course of events ought to count as an introduction, even if no formal vote on the ordinance was held.

The General Rule

After the day of introduction, an ordinance may be adopted by an affirmative vote equal to at least a majority of the council membership. (The mayor is not counted in determining council membership unless he or she was elected by and from the council.) Vacancies do not affect the number necessary for approval in this vote. If a member is properly excluded from voting on a particular issue, however, the number required for approval is a majority of the number of members not excused (see "Excusing Members from Voting," below). For example, a six-member council normally requires an affirmative vote of four members to adopt an ordinance. But if one member is excused on a particular issue, the council is treated as having only five members on that issue, and only three need vote affirmatively for that measure to pass. Table 8.1, below, sets out the required majority (and two-thirds) vote in the variously-sized city councils in North Carolina.

As noted above, the mayor is not counted in determining how many members constitute the council unless he or she is elected by and from the council. If a tie occurs, however, the mayor's tie-breaking vote is counted in determining whether the requisite majority vote was attained. Recall the example of the six-member council: if it divides three-to-three on an issue and the mayor votes affirmatively to break the tie, the measure has received the four votes necessary for adoption.

It should be noted that this sort of majority is required on a few *measures* in addition to ordinances. For example, G.S. 160A-75 requires the same vote procedures for adopting

- any action with the effect of an ordinance, no matter how labeled;
- any measure other than the budget ordinance or a project ordinance (or an amendment of either) that authorizes or commits the expenditure of funds; and
- any measure that authorizes, makes, or ratifies a contract.

Table 8.1 Required Votes in Different-Sized City Councils

Number of Council Members	Two-Thirds Vote	Majority Vote
11	8	6
9	6	5
8	6	5
7	5	4
6	4	4
5	4	3
4	3	3
3	2	2
2	2	2

Franchises

G.S. 160A-76 establishes a special voting rule for ordinances that grant, renew, extend, or amend a franchise, such as for a telephone company or a taxicab company. Such an ordinance—and franchise actions may be taken only by ordinance—is not finally adopted until it has been passed twice, at two separate regular meetings of the council.

Budget and Project Ordinances

G.S. 159-17 sets out a special rule for adopting and amending the annual budget ordinance and any capital project or grant project ordinances. These measures may be adopted by a simple majority of those present and voting, as long as a quorum is present.

Resolutions and Motions

Except as noted in the discussion on the general rule for adopting ordinances, the general law sets no voting requirements for adopting measures other than ordinances. (Some city charters do require that resolutions or other actions receive the same vote as ordinances.) For such measures, the rule is that action may be taken by a majority of those present and voting, so long as a quorum is present. Thus, if a council has eight members, its quorum is five; if only five members are present, a resolution or motion can be adopted by a vote of only three of the five.

Excusing Members from Voting

Conflicts of Interest

In general, council members must vote on all matters that come before the council. G.S. 160A-75, however, establishes an exception to that general rule in two circumstances in which there is a potential conflict of interest: when the question involves the council member's own financial interest, or when it involves his or her official conduct. (Note that the statute does not allow a council member to be excused in other circumstances that might also be thought to involve a conflict, such as when the matter before the council involves a relative of a council member.) A member's financial interest—by far the more common cause of a potential conflict—might be involved in such matters as the city's entering into a contract with a company in which the council member has an interest or regulating a business owned by the council member. (G.S. 160A-75 specifically provides that consideration of changes in council members' own compensation and allowances does not involve their own financial interest.) An example of a matter involving a member's official conduct would be consideration of a recall petition directed at a particular council member, as is possible under a handful of city charters. If either circumstance applies, a council member should refrain not only from voting, but also from participating in any way in the deliberations leading up to the vote.

Unfortunately, G.S. 160A-75 is somewhat ambiguous in its phrasing, leaving unclear the matter of whether it prohibits a council member from voting in the specified circumstances or simply permits a council member to be excused from voting in those circumstances. My own view is that the statute (1) recognizes that council members are prohibited from voting in certain circumstances (when some law other than G.S. 160A-75 prohibits voting) and (2) states that in those circumstances the council members are excused from voting. In addition, there may be other circumstances—still involving a member's financial interests or official conduct—in which some other law does not mandate abstention. In that circumstance, G.S. 160A-75 permits, but does not require, a council to excuse the member involved from voting and participating. The following paragraphs elaborate on this view.

Other Circumstances

There are three, probably four, general circumstances in which the law, apart from G.S. 160A-75, prohibits a council member from voting: in zoning ordinance amendments when the council member has a financial interest; in zoning-related quasi-judicial proceedings when due process prohibits the council member from participating or voting; when the city is considering contracting with a business owned by the council member; and (although this is less clear), when the common law establishes the prohibition.

First, G.S. 160A-381(d) prohibits a council member from voting on any zoning map or text amendment when the outcome is "reasonably likely to have a direct, substantial, and readily identifiable financial impact on the member." This statutory prohibition is a restatement of the general rule of G.S. 160A-75 made applicable to one sort of council action.

Second, city councils often act in a quasi-judicial manner, such as when they approve conditional use permits or other development permissions. When a council is acting quasi-judicially, constitutional due process can prohibit a member from participating and voting. This constitutional requirement has been incorporated into G.S. 160A-388(e1), which prohibits any member of any board exercising quasi-judicial functions related to land use regulations from participating in a proceeding on such matters if doing so would violate "affected persons' constitutional rights to an impartial decision maker." Although this constitutional and statutory rule clearly reaches the sort of financial conflicts at issue in G.S. 160A-75, the rule goes well beyond financial conflicts. The statute provides that impermissible conflicts "include, but are not limited to, a member having a fixed opinion prior to hearing the matter that is not susceptible to change, undisclosed ex parte communications, a close familial, business, or other associational relationship with an affected person, or a financial interest in the outcome of the matter."

Third, G.S. 14-234 establishes a general prohibition on contracts between local elected officials and the units they serve. The statute includes several exceptions, but each of the exceptions requires that the official with the conflict abstain from participating in or voting on any contract within the exception.

Finally, the common law historically has barred local elected officials from voting on matters that affect their personal financial interests. In *Kendall v. Stafford*, the North Carolina Supreme Court rejected an attempt by the Greensboro city council to increase council member salaries, writing that

> [t]he public policy of the State, found in the statutes and judicial decisions, has been pronounced against permitting one to sit in judgment on his own cause, or to act on a matter affecting the public when he has a direct pecuniary interest, and this is a principle of the common law which has existed for hundreds of years.[3]

Although the *Kendall* case is close to a century old, the state supreme court cited it some twenty years ago in discussing whether local elected officials may vote on legislative issues in which they have a direct personal financial interest. Although the court's discussion was

---

3. 178 N.C. 461, 464, 101 S.E. 15, 16 (1919).

dicta, its clear view was that nonparticipation is required in legislative decisions. In *County of Lancaster v. Mecklenburg County*, the court wrote that

> [w]ith legislative zoning decisions, an elected official with a direct and substantial financial interest in a zoning decision may not participate in making that decision. . . . Where there is a specific, substantial, and readily identifiable financial impact on a member, nonparticipation is required.[4]

Thus, it seems probable that some sort of common law prohibition on such voting continues, and that G.S. 160A-75 recognizes that prohibition. Unfortunately, the exact contours of any common law prohibition are unclear, and it is not always possible to advise officials whether or not a particular situation falls within the prohibition. The prudent course is probably to err on the side of abstention. Even if a conflict is not sufficient to prohibit a council member from voting, it will probably be enough to support a council's discretionary action in permitting the council member to abstain.

Unexcused Abstentions

Unless a council member is excused, either by the remaining members of the council or by action of law, he or she must vote; unexcused abstentions are not permitted. If an unexcused member still declines to vote, G.S. 160A-75 directs that he or she be counted as voting "Aye."

The rules for mayors are slightly different. If a mayor is elected by and from the council, he or she remains a council member and must vote. The same is true of a mayor whose city's charter requires the mayor to vote on all issues. But a mayor who may vote only to break a tie may choose not to vote at all in a tie. The rule against unexcused abstentions does not apply to the mayor in such a case. (Should the mayor refuse to break a tie, the measure is defeated.)

What about the member who leaves a meeting without being excused? We have seen that he or she continues to be counted as present for purposes of a quorum. In addition, G.S. 160A-75 directs that the member be counted as voting "Aye" on all questions that come before the council after he or she leaves.

---

4. 334 N.C. 496, 511, 434 S.E.2d 604, 614 (1993) (footnote, citations omitted).

Secret or Written Ballots

Voting by secret ballot is prohibited by the state's open meetings law, G.S. 143-318.13(b). If members sign their ballots, however, a council may vote by written ballot. Occasionally, a council may wish to conduct a vote—for example, to fill a vacancy—and members may not want to share how they voted until the vote is concluded. Signed written ballots permit such a procedure.

Voting by Proxy

North Carolina law provides no authority for voting by proxy on a city council or on any other board in state or local government.

The Open Meetings Law

A city council (as well as all other boards and commissions within city government) is a "public body" within the North Carolina open meetings law, which is codified as G.S. Chapter 143, Article 33C. The law applies to any "official meeting" of a public body, which is defined in G.S. 143-318.10(d) as any meeting or gathering—in person or electronically—of a majority of the members of a public body "for the purpose of conducting hearings, participating in deliberations, or voting upon or otherwise transacting the public business . . . of the public body." The public body must, as described earlier, give public notice of its official meetings, and those meetings must then be generally conducted in public. The law does, however, permit a public body to hold closed sessions, excluding the public, for a limited list of purposes:

- To prevent the disclosure of information that is privileged or confidential pursuant to state or federal law.
- To prevent the premature disclosure of an honorary degree, scholarship, prize, or similar award.
- To consult with an attorney in order to preserve the attorney-client privilege between the public body and the attorney.
- To discuss matters related to the location or expansion of industries or other businesses in the area served by the public body.

- To establish the public body's position in negotiating material terms in a contract to acquire real estate or in an employment contract.
- To consider the qualifications, competence, performance, character, fitness, conditions of employment, or conditions of initial employment of an individual public officer or employee; or to hear or investigate a complaint, charge, or grievance by or against an individual public officer or employee.
- To plan, conduct, or hear reports concerning investigations of alleged criminal misconduct.
- To discuss or take action regarding plans to protect public safety as it relates to existing or potential terrorist activity.

If a public body or some of its members violate the open meetings law, any person may bring an action seeking declaratory or injunctive relief. In addition, any person may bring an action to have declared invalid actions taken in proceedings in which a public body is found to have violated the open meetings statute.

Parliamentary Rules

G.S. 160A-71(c) permits a city council to adopt its own rules of procedure, as long as they are consistent with law and with generally accepted principles of parliamentary procedure. Probably the principal benefit of adopted rules is that they establish an orderly framework for council debate that still permits full participation and discussion among the members. Thus, for example, the rules could establish the circumstances under which various procedural motions are appropriate—and which motion must be voted on first. It should be noted that procedural rules adopted by a council are intended to facilitate the work of that council, not to give an additional ground upon which someone may challenge council action. The general rule is that violation of a council-adopted procedural rule does not have any effect on the validity of council action.[5]

Minutes

G.S. 160A-72 requires that a council, through the city clerk, keep "full and accurate" minutes of its proceedings. Although the statute does not detail what "full and accurate"

---

5. *See, e.g.,* Smith v. City of Dubuque, 376 N.W.2d 602 (Iowa 1985).

minutes should include, the proper content of council minutes is suggested by their purpose. That purpose is to provide an official record, or proof, of council actions. Therefore, at a minimum, the minutes should include two sorts of material. First, the actions taken by a council should be stated specifically enough to be identifiable and provable. For example, the minutes should include the text of each ordinance, resolution, and motion, or a cross-reference to some other location, such as an ordinance book, where that text can be found. Second, the minutes should include proof of any conditions necessary to action, such as the presence of a quorum. Anything more, such as a more or less verbatim account of what is said at a meeting, may be desired by a council but is legally unnecessary.

As noted above, the purpose of meeting minutes is to provide an official record and proof of council action. In a judicial proceeding, the minutes are the only evidence allowed of council action, and, as such, they may not be attacked on the ground that they are incorrect.[6] Once approved, the minutes may be modified in only two ways. First, a person may bring a legal action alleging that the minutes are incorrect and seeking a court order to correct them.[7] Second, and much more common, a council may itself modify its minutes if it finds that they are incorrect.[8]

Ordinance Books and Codes

Adopted resolutions, orders, and motions need only be set out in the council's minutes. Ordinances, however, must also be set out in an ordinance book and perhaps an ordinance code.

Ordinance Books

G.S. 160A-78 requires that all cities maintain an ordinance book, separate from the council minute books, in which all ordinances are placed when adopted. The purpose of this requirement is to provide convenient access to all ordinances without a laborious search of the minutes of a meeting from some distant past. If a city has codified its ordinances (see below), an ordinance stays in the ordinance book from the time it is adopted until it is codified. Most codes are updated every three or six months. If a city has not codified its ordinances, the ordinance stays in the ordinance book permanently. In either event, the ordinance book may be as simple as a loose-leaf notebook setting out ordinances in the

---

6. *See, e.g.*, State v. Baynes, 222 N.C. 425, 23 S.E.2d 344 (1942).
7. Hearne v. Stanly Cnty., 188 N.C. 45, 123 S.E. 641 (1924).
8. *See, e.g.*, Norfolk S. R.R. v. Forbes, 188 N.C. 151, 124 S.E. 132 (1924).

order of their adoption. The only substantive requirement is that the book be indexed in some manner.

Ordinance Codes

G.S. 160A-77 requires cities with populations of more than 5,000—and permits smaller cities—to codify their ordinances. A code is a compilation of a city's ordinances, systematically arranged by subject into chapters or articles. Typically, in the process of initial codification, a city will remove conflicts between ordinances adopted at different times and adopt new ordinances common to cities of comparable size. A city code is the city's parallel to the North Carolina General Statutes. In requiring larger cities to codify, the law assumes that these cities will have so many ordinances that particular ones would be difficult to locate in a simple ordinance book. If a city of fewer than 5,000 persons finds itself with a high number of ordinances, it, too, should codify those ordinances. A number of private firms offer codification services to cities.

It is crucial that a city place its ordinances in either an ordinance book or an ordinance code. Unless an ordinance is found in one or the other of these volumes, G.S. 160A-79 does not permit a court to enforce it. An ordinance that does not appear in an ordinance book or code effectively does not exist.

9 Public Comment and Public Hearings

Citizens enjoy two sorts of rights to address a city council. The first is to appear during a statutorily-required public comment period. The second is to appear at a public hearing.

Public Comment Periods

Section 160A-81.1 of the North Carolina General Statutes (hereinafter G.S.) requires each city council to provide at least one public comment period a month at a regular meeting. This is a time slot on the council's agenda during which any person may speak to the council on a topic of the speaker's choice. The statute itself does not set any rules for public comment, but it does allow the council to adopt reasonable rules regulating the public comment period.

Public Hearings

A variety of North Carolina statutes require that a city council hold a public hearing on certain matters before acting on those matters. In North Carolina, the public hearing required by statute is the exception rather than the rule. For example, no hearing is required before a council may adopt most ordinances or before it may levy a tax other than the property tax. With respect to other actions taken under state law, a city council may hold a public hearing if it wishes, but it need not do so. Federal statutes also occasionally require that cities hold public hearings.

G.S. 160A-81 sets out a number of rules governing the conduct of public hearings. These rules, set out just below, apply only to those hearings required by state law. A council probably enjoys greater flexibility with respect to other hearings it holds on its own initiative.

Location

A public hearing may be held anywhere within the city or within the county or counties in which the city is located.

Conduct of a Hearing

A council may adopt any rules it finds useful for assuring a smoothly run hearing, so long as those rules are fundamentally fair. G.S. 160A-81 specifically permits rules setting a maximum time for speakers, requiring large groups of citizens to designate spokespeople, and—when the crowd is too large for the room—requiring that groups designate delegates to represent them in the council chamber.

Continuing a Hearing

The statutes that require public hearings usually also require that public notice or advertisement be given of each hearing. But if a hearing is not completed on the scheduled day, is further advertisement required? G.S. 160A-81 sets out special rules for two situations:

1. If a hearing is held pursuant to a public notice and the hearing cannot be completed on the day scheduled, the council may recess the hearing until a specific, later day and time. If it does this, no further notice is necessary.
2. If a hearing is scheduled for a particular time but cannot be held because a quorum of the council is not present, the hearing is automatically rescheduled for the time of the next regular council meeting. Again, no further public advertisement is necessary in this scenario.

10 Possible Liabilities of Mayors and Council Members

Self-Dealing

Since 1825, North Carolina law has made it a misdemeanor for a public official to contract in his or her private capacity with the unit that he or she serves. (In addition, any contract entered into in violation of the statute, Section 14-234 of the North Carolina General Statutes (hereinafter G.S.) is void.) This means that a council member cannot contract in his or her private capacity to provide goods or services to the city that he or she serves. In its current statutory form, G.S. 14-234 also applies to contracts with a mayor or council member's spouse.

There are several exceptions to the statute's basic prohibition on contracting:

1. Any contract between the city and a bank or similar institution or with a regulated public utility.
2. Any interest in property conveyed by mayor or council member or his or her spouse to the city pursuant to a judgment, including a consent judgment, in a condemnation proceeding brought by the city.
3. Any employment relationship between the city and the spouse of the mayor or a council member.
4. Contracts in a cumulative amount of no more than $40,000 annually between a mayor or council member or their spouses and the city, when the city's population does not exceed 15,000. This exception does not apply to contracts for which competitive bidding is required under G.S. Chapter 143, Article 8—that is, construction contracts and purchase contracts over a minimum amount, currently $30,000.

If the city wishes to assert any of these exceptions, the mayor or council member involved may not participate in the council deliberations or vote on the matter.

Other Criminal Liabilities

G.S. 14-234 is one of a series of criminal offenses set out in G.S. Chapter 14, Article 31, Misconduct in Public Office. In general, most of the other statutes are very old and are rarely, if ever, the occasion for current prosecutions. Nevertheless, the following provisions are applicable to mayors and council members:

- G.S. 14-229 prohibits acting as a public officer before qualifying for the office by taking and subscribing the oath of office and by giving bond when applicable. Violation is a misdemeanor, and the person is to be ejected from the office.
- G.S. 14-230 prohibits a public officer from willfully omitting, neglecting, or refusing to discharge the duties of his or her office. Violation is a misdemeanor; if it is proved that the violator acted with a corrupt intent, he or she is also to be ejected from the office.
- G.S. 14-234.1 prohibits a public officer from using for personal gain any confidential information acquired in his or her official capacity. Violation is a misdemeanor.
- G.S. 14-247 and -248 prohibit using publicly-owned vehicles for a private purpose or repairing or supplying any private vehicle at public expense. Violation is a misdemeanor. (These last two sections are made applicable to city officials by G.S. 14-252.)

Civil Liability

Public officials and employees potentially face two basic areas of civil liability: tort liability under North Carolina law and liability under federal law for violations of the Civil Rights Act of 1871 (often referred to as Section 1983 because of its placement in the United States Code).

Tort Liability under North Carolina Law

Tort law protects bodily security, tangible property, financial resources, and reputation. A tort is a civil wrong, the parameters of which have been defined by centuries of court decisions. These decisions define the duties that one member of society owes to another, and the failure of one person to meet such a duty exposes that person to a claim for compensation by any person harmed by that failure. The purposes of tort law are to shift the cost of certain harms—torts—from the victim to the perpetrator, and, by requiring compensation, to deter persons from committing those harms.

At-a-Glance: Potential Liabilities for Mayors and Council Members		
Areas of Liability	**Prohibited Behavior**	**Classification/Penalty**
Self Dealing	• Contracting in private capacity with city unit served	Misdemeanor; contract void
Misconduct in Public Office	• Acting as public officer before taking oath	Misdemeanor; ejection from office
	• Willfully omitting/ neglecting/ refusing to discharge duties	Misdemeanor; ejection from office if corrupt intent shown
	• Using confidential information obtained while in office for personal gain	Misdemeanor

	• Misuse of public vehicles
	  ◦ Use for private purpose
	  ◦ Repair/supply private vehicle at public expense
		Misdemeanor

There are two major categories of torts, and the rules about public official liability differ as between the two categories. The first is intentional torts, which are deliberate wrongful acts that cause personal injury or property damage. Important examples of intentional torts include assault, battery, false imprisonment, and defamation. The second encompasses unintended actions that lead to injury or damage, which are included within the broad category of negligence. The law of negligence imposes a duty on all persons, including public officials and employees, to use reasonable care in conducting their daily activities. If a person fails to use reasonable care—i.e., is negligent—and as a result a second person suffers bodily harm or property damage, the victim is entitled to compensation from the negligent actor.

What constitutes an intentional tort is fairly clear, having been well-defined by decades of case law from the North Carolina courts and elsewhere. What constitutes negligence, on the other hand, is infinitely variable, and the decision as to whether specific conduct was negligent is made by the jury empaneled in each specific case in which a lawsuit is brought and reaches the trial stage.

Liabilities and Immunities of Mayors and Council Members

There is no immunity for a public officer or employee who commits an intentional tort in the course of his or her public work. The courts have decided that there is no strong public policy served by granting public actors immunity from liability for damages caused by intentional wrongful acts.

It is different, however, when a public official is charged with acting negligently. In that instance, there are important immunities that the courts have created to protect such officials as they carry out their work. One type of immunity that protects mayors and council members is absolute, while a second is considered qualified.

The grant of immunity that is absolute is known as *legislative immunity*, and it applies to any public official exercising legislative powers during the course of actually enacting or adopting legislation. Thus, there can be no personal liability for a mayor or council member because he or she voted to adopt an ordinance, even if the person acted with bad faith.

In all other activities, mayors and council members, because they are clearly public officials within the tort law definition of that term, are protected from liability for negligence by a *qualified public official immunity*. This immunity remains in place unless a plaintiff can prove that an official acted with malice, for corrupt reasons, or outside the scope of his or her official duties. These are difficult matters to prove, and as a result, it is very difficult to recover damages for negligent actions against mayors and council members (and other public officials) arising during their public activities.

Liability under Federal Law

Section 1983 of the Civil Rights Act of 1871 permits a person who has been harmed because a local government or its officers or employees violated his or her federal constitutional or statutory rights to sue the local government or the offending officer(s) or employee(s) and recover damages. Among the sorts of constitutional rights that have occasioned suits under this statute are the First Amendment's protections of free speech, the right to assemble, and freedom of religion; the Fourth Amendment's protections against unreasonable search and seizure; and the Fourteenth Amendment's protections against violations of due process or equal protection. Like common law tort liability under state law, this federal statute serves both to compensate victims of unconstitutional actions and to deter such actions by government officials and employees.

As with the common law, the federal statute offers two sorts of immunity from personal liability. The first is an absolute immunity for legislative actions that extends to local government officials with legislative powers. However, the immunity only reaches actual legislative actions, such as adopting ordinances, and does not include the various administrative activities undertaken by mayors and council members. The second category of immunity is qualified but nevertheless broad. It applies unless the official or employee's action violates clearly established statutory or constitutional rights that a reasonable person should have known about.

Insurance Coverage

Even if an official enjoys immunity from suit, whether under either state or federal law, it can be expensive to defend a lawsuit to the point of obtaining a dismissal because of the immunity. To help protect against that cost of litigation, and against the possibility of damages when the immunities do not apply, local governments typically obtain insurance that protects their governing board members and other officers and employees (as well as the government itself) from heavy personal expenditures.

Appendix 1. Principal General Laws Affecting City Government

General Statutes Chapter 160A. This chapter is the basic city government law for North Carolina. It provides authority for most of the functions that cities engage in and grants most of their regulatory powers.

General Statutes Chapter 153A. This chapter is the basic county government law for North Carolina, paralleling Chapter 160A. It is mentioned here because a few of its authorizations—particularly for libraries and ambulance services—extend to cities as well as counties.

General Statutes Chapter 159. This chapter regulates local government finance—budgeting, fiscal control, and borrowing.

General Statutes Chapter 105. This chapter authorizes both state and local governments to levy taxes. The local taxes covered by this chapter are the property tax, the sales and use tax, and the privilege license tax.

General Statutes Chapter 143. This chapter is largely devoted to state government, but it also includes the local government purchasing statute (Article 8) and the open meetings law (Article 33C).

General Statutes Chapter 132. This chapter regulates access to public records.

General Statutes Chapter 163, Subchapter IX. This subchapter is the municipal elections law.

Appendix 2. Suggested Reading

For those readers interested in more detailed information about city government in North Carolina, the following School of Government publications may be of interest.

Local Government Board Builders Series

See the list of other books in the *Board Builders* series at the front of this publication.

Other School of Government Publications

Lawrence, David M. (ed.). *County and Municipal Government in North Carolina*. Chapel Hill, NC: UNC School of Government, 2007 (2nd edition forthcoming).

Bell, A. Fleming, II. *Suggested Rules of Procedure for a City Council*. 3rd ed. Chapel Hill, NC: UNC School of Government, 2000.

Bell, A. Fleming, II. *Ethics, Conflicts, and Offices: A Guide for Local Officials*. 2nd ed. Chapel Hill, NC: UNC School of Government, 2011.

Lawrence, David M. *Open Meetings and Local Governments in North Carolina: Some Questions and Answers*. 7th ed. Chapel Hill, NC: UNC School of Government, 2008.

Lawrence, David M. *Public Records Law for North Carolina Local Governments*. Chapel Hill, NC: UNC School of Government, 2009.

Owens, David. *Introduction to Zoning*. 3rd ed. Chapel Hill, NC: UNC School of Government, 2007 (new edition forthcoming).

Bluestein, Frayda. *An Overview of Contract Bidding Requirements for North Carolina Local Governments*. Chapel Hill, NC: UNC School of Government, 2007.

School of Government Blog

Coates' Canons: NC Local Government Law Blog offers a series of short explanations of legal issues, court cases, and proposed and new legislation affecting North Carolina local governments. The local government law faculty of the School of Government are the authors, and new entries are posted several times a week. The blog can be accessed at www.canons.sog.unc.edu.